The Kid From Kansas in the Marine Corps

The Life and Times of Robert F Paden, Volume 2

Robert F Paden

Published by The Plowman, 2022.

While every precaution has been taken in the preparation of this book, the publisher assumes no responsibility for errors or omissions, or for damages resulting from the use of the information contained herein.

THE KID FROM KANSAS IN THE MARINE CORPS

First edition. November 2, 2022.

ISBN: 979-8223777892

Written by Robert F Paden.

I dedicate this book to the officers and men who trained me to be a Marine and those who by their example and leadership, confirmed to me what a good and loyal Marine should be and what a man should be..

CHAPTER ONE
USMC BOOT CAMP

He was inches from my face, shouting at the top of his voice. WHAT'S YOUR NAME? Robert F Paden! SIR! Sir! WHAT? My name is Robert F Paden Sir! LISTEN, SKIN HEAD! WHEN I ASK WHO YOU ARE, YOU TELL ME YOUR NAME, RANK AND SERIEL NUMBER! WHO ARE YOU? Private Robert F Paden 1355745 Sir! DID YOU EVER PEA IN YOUR PANTS? Yes Sir! WHEN, YESTERDAY? When I was a little boy! SIR! Sir! WHAT? I peed in my pants when I was a little boy Sir! WHAT ARE YOU SMIRKING ABOUT? I wouldn't smirk, Sir!

With that, he left me and went down the line to try another guy. Our platoon was standing at attention after passing morning inspection. We had been warned that we were to stand at rigid attention, look straight ahead and answer every question in a clear, loud voice, without moving or changing expression on our face until we were dismissed. For some it was extremely difficult to see that this had a purpose and also that it would not last forever. I had passed that test! I knew from what he had told us in the beginning and from watching what happened to others that if I smiled, laughed, cried or flinched in reaction to his provocations, it would bring on extra calisthenics or some sort of sanction! They were teaching us to deal with stress.

That was Staff Sergeant Scarborough, one of our DI's (drill instructors) He told us the first day. "I'll be your mother, your father, you teacher, your everything for the weeks you will be in this camp. You will call me sir!

When I tell you to do something, you will say, yes sir! And do it and think later. Hopefully you will graduate from here, and you will be a Marine! You will be able to think for yourself, function under severe circumstances, and you will be a part of the United States Marines!!

On February 2, 1953 I signed up for Marine Corps Reserve Air Wing and started week-end training every 15 days, plus a two-week tour in California. That program was mostly classes on aircraft mechanics in theory and working with older aircraft mechanics. When we entered in to boot camp in July of that year however, we found out what the real Marine Corps was like!

It was tough, but I decided that an old farm boy could take it if anyone could; besides, this wasn't going to last forever. So right off I decided to keep my nose clean, say "yes sir!" and obey. I had learned to work on the farm at a very young age and knew what it was to work hard and put in long hours. I figured that if others could pass through "boot camp", I could too. The orders were many times hard but never impossible. I began to see their purpose; to take this bunch of green, rebellious, ignorant, wise-off, young boys and make obedient, strong and loyal Marines out of them.

The recruits were from all parts of society. Some were farm kids, usually in better shape than the city boys. One kid brought a set of golf clubs with him. The DI said, "I'll take care of those for you son. You won't be needing them for a while!" We were from all parts of society. Two of the boys in our outfit were American Indians. There were black boys, Italians, Mexicans and Caucasians. Some came from poor families and some came from rich families. But we became all alike. The DI's would tear us down. "You don't amount to anything, you snot nosed young panty waists!" We were herded into the barber shop where the barbers were waiting, poised by their chairs with big smiles. The first barber said, "How do you want your hair cut son?" All the barbers waited for the effect as the first boy said in some detail how he would like his hair cut. Immediately all the barbers went to work with their big, fast clippers and in about two minutes, three boys stepped out of the barber's chairs with their heads shining! "Next!" shouted the barbers and in a short time all of us had identical "haircuts". From then on, they called us "skin heads"! We were all the same, rich poor, black, white. We were all just "skin heads", recruits! There was no "affirmative action" necessary. We were all the same! No one felt proud when they ran us through the clinic naked examining every part of our body, then jabbed us in both buttocks to inject all the inoculations we were to receive!

The extremely rigorous training and lack of sleep also wore down all rebellion eventually. For the first two weeks we averaged four or five hours of sleep each night. When we ate, we had fifteen minutes to fall out from formation, go in the mess hall, pass down the line for them to fill our tray, sit down, eat and get back out to formation. Then march, march, march, run, run, run. When we had a fifteen-minute break, everybody would be asleep on the ground, even if it was rocky ground! But the food was good; the exercise evidently didn't hurt us. The skinny guys gained weight and you can guess what happened to the fat guys! One of my buddies pealed down from a flabby 240 to a trim 180 pounds! I gained weight!

Perhaps you could say their system of training amounts to brain washing or indoctrination but the purpose was not to change our spiritual life or American values, but to make good Marines out of us, which is what we signed up for! They were teaching us to stretch our bodies to greater extremes because in battle and in service, we would need the knowledge that a healthy young body can go a lot farther than normal, and even far beyond what one would imagine. I learned quickly to stand at attention, look straight ahead without changing my expression even while the DI was shouting in my face, trying his best to make me laugh or cry! Much of this rigor was teaching us to deal with stress. Not only were they stretching our bodies, they were also stretching our minds to understand that our limits are much higher that we had thought. Part and parcel of being a good Marine is to be a loyal American.

After the first phase, they began to teach us leadership, team leadership. For example, in a squad of four, one is in charge, the others follow, moving as one. But if the first man falls, the second takes charge immediately. If the second man falls the third man takes charge and so on. Leadership and obedience are married. Without one you can´t have the other. We had classes on leadership and unity as well. The underlying principle of both obedience and leadership is unity. _esprit de corps_, the Marine Corps motto means, "spirit of unity". It's the motivation in the members of a group to want the group to succeed. That, in the end, was one of the main purposes of boot camp! It's called "camp" because, "we are not staying here. We're moving on!

The sound of reveille was just the click of the light switch! Woe unto the recruit that does not hit the deck (floor) with his feet almost before the lights all come on! We had fifteen minutes to get out of the rack (bed), make it real tight! go to the head (bathroom), get shaved, get dressed, put away all gear and get out into formation! Those who didn't make it did all kinds of extra calisthenics. Everyone had to shave, even those who didn't have a beard yet had to scratch their face to show they had shaved.

Some tried to rebel and paid for it dearly. My good friend Johnny "fell down the stairs" and got banged up <u>twice.</u> He was a big guy and had never been beaten in a fight. Now, he couldn't seem to learn to simply say "yes sir!" and obey. In later years the Marines were heavily criticized for the hardness of Boot Camp, but all the Marines I knew that went on to serve their time of enlistment were in accord with the training they had received. I was, for sure. They taught us to work as a unit. In battle or in critical situations there can be no discord. Then there is no time for everyone to express his opinion. A unit has to move forward as one man if they are going to achieve their objective. The importance of loyalty to the unit, no matter how small or large it is, along with leadership, (responsibility), cannot be overstressed. Much later I learned how the self-centered slothfulness of just one man caused terrible damage and almost cost a pilot his life.

After the "breaking" of that rebellious will of youth, they began to encourage us. You can do it! Now you're a US Marine! Learning to march was part of that. An entire unit of 180 men all marching in perfect step, turning right, turning left, turning around. It's a beautiful thing to watch, 180 men, all moving as one man to the cadence of the sergeant. It's a column marching forward, suddenly it's a line moving sideways! Then the line divides in two, half going forward, the other half marching back till it becomes a double line. The group becomes a square, becomes a rectangle, again it's a column! All that is not only pretty for parades, every man learns to obey immediately and also to act as part of a unit! Each man was issued an M1 rifle. That same rifle went with me until I was discharged. I learned to take it apart, clean it and put it back together in short time. I liked the rifle range. I made sharpshooter the first time, and did better later on at the second range.

My previous time in the reserves was counted as part of my training as an aircraft mechanic. Besides the two week-ends per month, we had two weeks of maneuvers in California. And then, after Boot Camp I was stationed at that same base. El Toro Marine Air Base, close to Orange City and not far from Los Angeles, California. It was a Thriving Air Base at that time. Several fighter squadrons were stationed there. I was assigned to Headquarters Squadron. Headquarters Squadron was in charge of the CO's plane plus moving men and materials for all the fighter squadrons on the Base. Because of the urgent need of men, they were using what they called OJT, (on the job training) to continue our training instead of the full course in mechanic school.

So, I had been here before for two weeks with the reserve squadron. They were using a left-over World War II fighter, the F8 Grumman Bear Cat. It had been built to combat the Japanese Zero, which was small and much more maneuverable than our pre-World War II planes. I don't know if the Bear Cat ever made it into combat. It was built right at the end of the war.

That's when I had a "hairy" experience working on the flight line. I was green about working with airplanes, the young pilot who came out to fly this machine was also green, and the machine, the Bear Cat was very cantankerous and unpredictable. It had a huge piston engine and a four bladed prop (propeller) mounted on a short-coupled plane. My job was first to help the pilot pre check out the plane, help him get strapped in, then hold the fire bottle to make sure he got started and out of there safely.

After I got the pilot strapped in and was on the ground with fire bottle in hand, I gave him the thumbs up to start the engine. The pilot kicked in the crank and the high-powered engine coughed once, coughed twice, and <u>then caught on fire!</u> Those fighters used a very high-test gasoline and we had just filled it with gas! Suddenly fire was everywhere. I had never used a fire bottle before but of course knew how to jerk the pin out and start spraying the fire (supposedly to put it out quickly). The fire bottle was empty of the chemical to put out fires but still had gas. So here I was spraying that fire with air! The air from the bottle would make the flames go down, but they would immediately come up again when I moved on with the spray. I didn't know what was wrong. I kept going at it though, as the fire began licking up over the canopy with my new pilot trapped inside. Finally, someone else on the flight line came to our rescue with a fire bottle that worked and was able to put it out. The pilot was very grateful and wanted to recommend us for a medal. I was too embarrassed to want to be involved, feeling that I had failed. I never heard any more about it.

CHAPTER TWO
HEADQUARTERS SQUADRON

I was glad to get assigned to Headquarters Squadron where I immediately started OJT. One of my first assignments was search duty for downed planes. This could be any plane, civilian or military. Often our squadron was called upon to help search for lost planes. We used the little two engine Beech Craft for that service. So, I would sit by one of the windows and look out for the lost plane as we swooped into every valley and gulley and up over every hill in southern California. There was no glory or pleasure or reward in that job. We never found a lost plane, though we searched for several.

I did have one victory though in that duty. When I was a kid, I would always get car sick, so you might imagine how this kind of flying affected me! I would fight that motion sickness for the entire two-hour flight! I never threw up, but I was always so close to it that I would be like a wet rag when we finally landed! Then one morning as I was preflighting (inspecting the condition of the plane for flight) I stuck my head inside the plane and the smell made me feel sick. I thought, if just the smell makes me sick, then that means that it's in my head that I will get sick. If it's in my head then I'll deal with my head about that and get over it! And get over I did. Later on, in-flight duty, I could even pass out sick bags to passengers who were throwing up without getting sick myself! I never thought about it but they might have been testing me on those search jobs, to see if I could fly in those low flying, non-pressurized planes that are really rough riding, without getting sick!

According to my aptitude in tests I was assigned to work on AirFrame which has to do with all the delicate system of air controls. It was a real challenge to get all the components, flaps, ailerons, elevators, rudder and landing gear to respond perfectly. The landing gear of course was hydraulic, but the airframe controls were connected by cables. They all had to have exactly the right tension to transmit the commands of the pilot. I used a tension meter which I would clamp on each cable to test the tension. I had a chart that specified the tension that each cable should have. The tension had to be set on pairs of cables too, as the return cable will change with the its mate. This extensive revision check was done on the plane after each 240 flight hours. I was assigned to work on the air frame by myself. (My work had to pass the inspection and approval of the flight-line sergeant). It was a difficult and interesting job to make those flight controls to respond perfectly.

The sergeant major must have been happy with my work because soon after that he put me in charge of one of our transport planes as crew chief. That same sergeant helped me overcome motion sickness as well. (Avoid swallowing saliva on an empty stomach, keep busy and focused on your job in flight and believe you won't get sick and eat a steak dinner if possible before you go on a flight.) Being crew chief of that plane was the most exciting part of my tour of duty in El Toro. It was an R4D transport plane. Our squadron had four of them. As Headquarters Squadron we were in charge of the Commanding General's plane also, whose crew chief was a sergeant. I was the only PFC acting as crew chief. My plane had much more lowly duties like moving men and tools to different training bases around the country.

Actually, the job description "crew chief" sounds bigger than it is. In much larger planes or different circumstances there would be a crew, but in my case, I was chief of the crew of one! And Watashi (myself) was that crew! But I got to travel a lot and I was responsible for the plane while it was on a trip. My position in flight was right behind the pilot and co-pilot. On command I raised and lowered the flaps (for braking and lifting) raised and lowered the landing gear, turned on and off the windshield wipers, actuated the de-icing boots on the front of the wings and the de-icing fluid at the center of the props when we had icy conditions. (That would scare the daylights out of the passengers as the loosened ice would bang against the side of the airplane and some thought the plane was about to blow up!) In flight, I checked the cargo, making sure it hadn't shifted in takeoff and attended any of the passenger's needs. More than once I was obliged to pass out sick bags as these non-pressurized planes had to fly at 10 or 12 thousand feet where the air is very rough at times. It was not at all unusual for a passenger to get sick and throw up, and many times that would make others get sick. On one flight there were about 12 people and I think every one of them threw up. It was a real victory for me not to get sick too!

I made some bloopers on some of the first trips, like forgetting to remove the chocks (exterior control locks) when we were getting ready for takeoff. But the pilots helped me get over my greenness. Once a group of pilots organized a fishing trip (paid for by taxpayer money) and they took my plane. I couldn't go fishing with them because I had to watch over the plane and have it all ready to take off when they returned. I took my job seriously and on Sunday morning went out to get it fueled up and all ready to go on Monday. After fueling up, the truck driver left, and the small airfield seemed to be empty. Part of pre-flight could include starting up the engines and checking the gauges and "feathering" the props. (The props are made so that the angle of the blades can be changed to give it more bite as the plane gains speed and less bite when it's taking off) Well, I kind of got carried away with my check out and revved the engines up too much and with the prop pitch in "power mode" for takeoff! Suddenly I realized that the tail had come off the ground and the plane was trying to fly! (Fortunately, it was tied down.) I jerked the throttles back and the tail came down with a resounding thump! I looked at the tower to see if there were any red lights flashing or someone coming running out! Not a sign. Everyone was sleeping this Sunday morning! Only I and the plane knew about it and now you do also!

<u>My very first flight</u> as crew chief was very interesting. I had worked with others and knew the procedures but this was the first time that I was by myself and responsible for loading and caring for the plane. A fighter

squadron was moving from a desert air field back to home base after maneuvers. There was a problem that neither I nor the pilots knew about until we arrived at the desert air field, which was a two-hour flight from our home base. They had ordered three planes to pick up the supplies and only two planes were sent. The first plane was just leaving and had only taken about one third of the cargo, thinking there would be two more planes.

I must say a word about the pilot and co-pilot to better explain their attitude. They were both old "salts" who had served in World War II, "left overs" from a special breed. The pilot was a Light Coronel and the co-pilot was one of the few remaining flying sergeants (a special commission given near the end of the War.) The Light (Lieutenant) Coronel might have been a General but had been busted (demoted) because of his lack of obeying flight rules. Both pilots had many hours of flight time to their credit and were perhaps biding their time for retirement. They both had a super relaxed and confident attitude about flying these "Gooney Birds". All of which did not add up to their strict obedience to protocol.

When we were greeted with the news that there were really two plane loads left, the pilot turned to me (not knowing that I was new to all this) Paden, ya think yu ken load it all on? Well, "Paden" was not about to admit he couldn't do something at this point. "Yes sir!" I said with bravado on the outside and kind of a sweaty "it'll work out" inside! I thought, if they are willing to take it all on one load, so am I! I did remember the principle of loading the heavy weight over the wings, so I told the guys who helped load to bring me all the heavy stuff first, and bring they did because they were in a big hurry to get out of there. The plane's Marine Corps designation was R4D, originally called Douglas C47 (Air Force), or DC3 (civilian) built back in 1937. They were very dependable aircraft well known for their durability. Ours had been remodeled to Marine Corps specifications with a larger Wright engine, replacing the old Pratt Whitney, a larger four blade prop, larger square-tipped wings and a big square tail. We were proud of them.

We loaded the air compressors and other machinery and heavy tools first, and last of all, the sea bags (men's personal bags). The fuselage of the plane was so full that we had to pull out some of the sea bags in order for the pilots and myself to crawl in. I had to ask one of other men to hold the fire bottle for starting. The pilots would have started without the fire bottle. They weren't much for protocol you know. I was really sweating, and not just from the work! I was tense about doing my job in flight of operating those few controls, (my first flight) and my attention was riveted on one thing. Will this thing fly? To rub it in a little, the Coronel said casually, "Do you think it'll fly Paden?" I hope so sir, I croaked! Then he said, to assure me a little bit perhaps, as we were straightening out on the Landing Strip, "We have ten miles of strip here in the desert to find out!"

As he wound up the engines and checked the props in readiness to take off, I think I even tried to pray a little bit. I have no idea how much our load weighed, but it had to be heavy. The fuselage was completely full and a lot of it was iron. We start to roll. We picked up speed. I was so glad for those ten miles! But really, we didn't seem to go much longer than usual until the air speed indicator showed more than enough speed for normal take off. We began to fly! When the pilot gave me the sign for wheels up, I prayed again that we didn't suddenly fall out of the sky! But after we leveled off, he looked around at me and grinned, showing me the trim controls, "It trimmed up perfect Paden!" Of course, they had to land with much care because of the tremendous weight that might cause the landing gear to fold or blow a tire. But we made a perfect landing. Those pilots were very proud of the old "Gooney bird" as it was sometimes called in imitation of a former cargo plane. They told me later that one of the times he got busted was because he liked to show people how that plane would take off with only one engine!

One of my favorite duties was helping with the flight testing after each maintenance check. For some reason, they picked me to help on the flight testing of other planes, not normally assigned to me. The plane had to be put through every normal maneuver and then beyond "normal" flight condition to see if it would respond and stand the test. One of the most exciting maneuvers was the stall test. There were two different stall tests, the first was "softer" as the plane was made to climb at full power ever more steeply until it "mushed out" (lost ability to fly). That was exciting but the pilots seemed to be always in control. The second test was to pull back the throttles in level flight and let the plane slow down on its own. Everything would be silent, the engines turning over slowly. Our air speed would be slower and slower until the plane would "tremble" ¡And suddenly become a rock, falling out of the sky! We had enough altitude of course that they could regain control and level out again but those first seconds were enough to get anyone's heart up in his throat!

Since we flew in all kinds of weather, we often came in to land with little or no visibility. In southern California it was often very foggy. Since our planes didn't have radar, we had to come in by GCA (Ground Control Approach). For me it was exciting but also fascinating because of the need for perfect coordination between the pilot and ground control operator, who was in the control tower with the radar screen in front of him and our plane on the screen. I also had earphones, so I could hear all the conversation between the tower and the pilots. At about 20 miles out the pilot and ground controller (who was sitting in the tower with the radar screen in front of him) would be in constant contact. From my position behind the pilots, I could see out the windshield. The windshield wipers were usually going full speed, as even if it wasn't raining, the fog would be so heavy that water would form on the windshield. Many times, we were completely blind, only fog or rain. The controller would advise the speed and altitude, at 15 miles out he would start saying more exactly what speed and altitude he wanted. At ten miles out he would start a one-way conversation, and literally take charge of the flight. So, I would hear, *"on glide path…two degrees left, one degree down, on glide path, one degree right, three quarter flaps down* (that was my control) *on glide path, wheels down* (my control) *full flaps down"*. Sometimes just seconds before touch down he would say, "You should see the landing lights now, and suddenly the lights would appear and we would be very close to the strip and touch down. Sometimes it would be raining but more often fog. There is no fog as thick as the fog of southern California! We never had a bad landing on GCA and I loved it!

One pilot hated it though. He was an office man and only flew the six hours per month that he was required to fly to keep up his pilot status. He was flying alone in a Beechcraft and in that practice, he had to put up blinders that clipped in front of the pilot, so that he was forced to depend on the controller. But the SOP (Standard Operating Procedure) was that the controller would tell him to take off the blinds well before he would touch down. The controller forgot to tell him to take the blinders off and he suddenly hit the ground without expecting it! It scared the daylights out of him and was he ever mad! I wonder if the controller didn't do that on purpose because the pilot was and "office pinky"!

"LIBERTY"

Johnny Norris, my old high school buddy was stationed at LTA (Lighter Than Air). They worked with Air balloons, which was not far from my station, El Toro. Sometimes we would have a weekend pass together. We both had relatives living in Southern California and often would visit one of them, "mooching" or "free-loading" off of them. One Saturday night we went to a dance in Anaheim. Nothing particularly exciting happened at the dance. When we came out of the parking lot onto the street, it was extremely foggy as many times happened in that area. On the street I turned left instead of right. We went for about two hours straining to see a street or highway that we recognized. Nothing! Finally, we came to the agonizing conclusion that we had gone all that way north instead of south. Now we had to go all that way back! We turned around. It was daylight when we got back to the base!

One night I was in a rough part of downtown Los Angeles by myself hitch hiking back to the base. A car stopped to pick me up. It was full of young guys about my age. After I got in the car, I perceived right away that they were thinking about "rolling" me. (Beating and robbing) There were reports that this had happened several times in the past few weeks. They were talking excitedly in Spanish which I didn't understand. Since I was in uniform (Marine), I thought I just might be able to bluff my way out of this. I was ready to give them a run for their money, but they had me outnumbered five to one! So, I began to brag about my exploits in fights and how I left my adversaries out on the ground! Pretty soon they stopped the car and asked me to get out which I did with a lot of bravado but inside really glad to be out of there!

Another time, I'd had a few beers and my tooth started to ache, so I decided to stop by the dentist on duty when I came back on base. He took me right in, but told me he didn't have any anesthesia. He said, "Can you take a little pain?" Sure! What was this Marine going to say? Well. It was a lot more than a <u>little</u> pain! But, do you think I was going to yell? I was cold sober when I walked out of there.

I got to thinking later; maybe that Doc thought, "He thinks he's tough? We'll see!" (I think the Doc was Navy to boot.)

I think it was on about our first week-end pass that Johnny and I went to the beach. For some reason the beach was just about deserted. It was a cloudy day and we would swim a while and then lay out on the sand, then jump in the water again and then dry off on the sand. Since it was cloudy, we didn't worry about getting sunburned. How wrong could we be! I was burned so badly that the next day, it was difficult to walk. It's a Court Marshall offense in the service to get sun-burned so badly that you can't work. I don't know how Johnny survived at his base, but I suffered through a week of agony silently! To take a shower, every drop was like someone throwing rocks at me! Needless to say, from then on, I had more respect for salt water and cloudy days!

CHAPTER THREE
"VMF 235"

I took leave in September of 1954. I had planned to get home in time for the wheat harvest but couldn't get leave till September. But the weather had been really dry and there had been no harvest. I drove back to California by myself and started out from Denver in the afternoon. As I topped the continental divide, it started snowing. If my memory serves me right it was Vail Pass. The sun was just going down. There was no traffic on the road. The snow came straight down in great white flakes. The road became one white blanket without lines. The heavy flakes coming down almost made me dizzy. I could barely tell where the side of the road was. On one side the mountain rose above and on the other it dropped off. The car wasn't slipping but it was pushing snow in front of the tires on those winding mountain roads. There were no other cars or trucks on the road. At that time the highway was only two lanes. For hours I traveled, quite slowly but never stopping. I got in to Grand Junction in the early morning hours and filled up the gas tank, thankful that I hadn't run out of gas. I had planned to rent a hotel and sleep, but now I was wide awake so decided to keep going. I stopped at a breakfast place and had some pancakes and coffee, then went on my journey. I decided to hold the car at 60 miles an hour steady and it turned out that I made better time than when, at other times, I had driven faster, but had not carefully controlled my speed. I got in to LA that night. I rented a cheap hotel room but couldn't sleep. I had been running on adrenaline and it wouldn't let me relax.

When I checked back in to El Toro, I found I had been transferred to Fighter Squadron VMF235. They were getting ready to go on gunnery practice in southern California near the rural town of El Centro. It's an irrigated valley with water from the Colorado River, which also fills the Hoover Dam in Nevada on its way south. El Centro farms produce alfalfa. Every day the temperature was about 115%! The air was dry as a bone. Alfalfa thrives in hot weather as long as it has lots of water, and at that point they had plenty of water. They were getting eight cuttings per year, in comparison to what we used to get in Colorado, three or maybe four if the frost held off. Here in El Centro Valley, it's always summer.

I was assigned to plane number 7, the "FJ2" that was my plane until I was discharged. They gave us permission to go without shirts working on the flight line and no one got a sunburn! The barracks were very old wooden structures but had air conditioning and we slept well at night.

For the pilots to practice their gunnery skills they tie a painted nylon cloth the size of a plane to the tow plane with a long nylon rope. It's pulled behind the lead plane for the other planes to shoot at it out over the desert. When the tow plane takes off, the long nylon rope stretches like a rubber band, the target lags behind, then begins to catch up to the plane as the elasticity overcomes the drag. It's very interesting. Our job was just to keep the planes fueled up and repaired. We didn't have "liberty" there so I didn't get to know the people or the farms which always interest me. The gunnery practice lasted two weeks.

Going to and from El Centro from El Toro, we were given the option of taking the military bus or taking our own car. One of the guys had a Packard car. My only knowledge of Packard's was that they were a big expensive cars and looked something like and old Rolls Royce. They were always black and for old rich people. This guy was a real Packard enthusiast and I began to be quite amazed at the quality and precision of that car. That engine would turn up to over 5000 RPM and sound as smooth as a kitten. It was completely stable on the road at high speeds. I don't remember what speed it got up to. The RPM was what impressed me the most I guess.

Other than being able to drive at very high speeds without a patrolman stopping us, the desert route was mostly uneventful. We did pass two interesting things; the Salten Sea which is below sea level, and Twenty Nine Palms, a rich man's town out there on the desert. All the houses are white stucco with pink tile roofs. It's an oasis in the middle of the desert. Their source of money back then without internet etc. was probably big bank accounts.

THE HIGH SEAS

Our outfit was being shipped overseas and we were to go by ship. Our planes were packed in cosmolin a thick rubbery material that is sprayed on to cover every exposed part of the plane from rusting while being shipped across the waters. The ship that transported them overseas was a small World War II carrier that had been decommissioned from being a combat carrier and was now being used as a transport ship. I was disappointed that they sent me on the troop ship instead of that one.

Crossing the high seas is an experience. Every continent has a shelf that goes out into the ocean before it drops down to the "deep". That of course varies with each coast but is pretty much true in the whole world. Once the ship gets off the continental shelf, the face and mood of the sea change completely. The water no longer just has waves. It has mountains and valleys. The sea is always rolling. Even big ships roll around in the sea. We shipped out to Japan from the port in San Diego. Most of the sailors on that trip got sick. It would have been a little funny if it hadn't been so pathetic with the sailors hanging over the rails and heaving in the heads (bathrooms). It so happened that for most of the sailors on this ship, it was the first time they had crossed the ocean. When we came on board, they laughed at us saying, "you guys are gonna get really sick when we get out to sea." They had been doing maneuvers on the continental shelf and hadn't yet seen the high seas. Since we were two complete squadrons, many of our men had been overseas before and others had done a lot of flying, and were more accustomed to motion than the new sailors were! Far less Marines got sick than sailors! It's a good thing too because we were really packed in, 3000 troops on board besides the crew of the ship.

The sleeping bay had long aisles, on both sides of each aisle were the sleeping racks (a canvas, hammock type bed with a fold up pipe frame), seven high. A fat man wouldn't have survived here! If the guy on top had thrown up, we would all have gotten it! There was barely room enough between one rack and the next one higher to squeeze into bed when the racks were down. At six o'clock sharp; I can still hear the call! Tata tatá (bugle) "Reveille, reveille, reveille! All hands up! Heave out and trice up! Clear out the main deck! Man your stations! All out for muster!" That was a call for the ship's crew as well, but for us it meant you've got to get out of bed, watch out for falling bodies from above and in that very cramped space, quickly make you rack and fold it up, put on your clothes, store your gear (bags), go to the bathroom and shave, and get your butt up for muster. We of course were not new recruits but we had to maintain discipline without exception.

On the first day, I volunteered for mess duty (kitchen). I wanted to keep busy to make the time pass more quickly. The kitchen had rows of huge pots, each one swiveled on a yoke hanging from a derrick so it could be easily be swung out from the fire and turned over to dump its contents into the big serving pots. Cooking for four thousand men had to be well organized! The chief cook was a sailor with "lots of time in grade" He always wore a cook's outfit so I never knew his rank. A colorful type, and very cheerful, of Chinese background, amiable and confident in this business of cooking huge amounts of food, he would have fit into any sea story! It's interesting that after all these years, his personality stands out in my memory more than anything else about that kitchen or my job while I was there except that I enjoyed working there.

The sea got rough. We hit a storm. The captain advised us that we would go right through the eye of the storm and be in it for about 4 days. It was so big that to go around it would mean going down all the way to Hawaii and add a week to our travel time. Even so, it was a two weeks trip to Japan. The reason for going through the eye of the storm is that the safest thing for a ship in a storm is to head directly into the wind as much as possible. Coming out on the other side of the storm was harder because to keep on course we had to quarter into the wind, making it hit us somewhat from the side. It was rough but as I found out the next year when we came back, it was mild compared to that storm. Coming back, I was working in the press office which was above deck and though the deck was at least 40 feet above water standing still, the waves washed another 15 feet above the deck when they washed across, leaving the main part of the ship under water for several moments. That storm came from every direction, sometimes from the side, sometimes straight on. The ship was very large, but sometimes the bow would come out of the water and you could hear the props rotating and when they hit the water again, the ship would lurch forward!

And now we are crossing toward the west; to arrive at the Far East! We also crossed the International Date Line and suddenly entered into tomorrow! When we came back, we entered into yesterday! (Don't worry about it; they had to put the date line somewhere.)

Two or three days out from Japan we began to see fishing boats. Entire families who pretty much live out their lives on the sea. I discovered later that they probably had come from the Aleutian Islands, so they weren't as far from land as I first imagined. But it still fascinates me thinking about these people who live such different lives than we know. When I visited Hong Kong much later, I saw where the fishermen come in to sell their wares and buy supplies. The bay, more than a half mile across was completely full of the fishing boats that had come in to sell their wares and buy supplies.

CHAPTER FOUR
JAPAN

Japan is small in size. From past time unknown, perhaps because of their need for more room, the Japanese culture was geared for war. Their folklore was all about war and the great warriors of their past. Through the 20's and 30's they waged war with China to get more land, but then that need evolved into greed for power. Their armies were extremely cruel. They subjugated the Province of Manchuria, China under an iron hand and their practices when they took over an area or took prisoners were atrocious. Americans, who were taken prisoner during World War II were subjected starvation and torture. During one prisoner exchange, the Japanese bombed both the American and their own prisoner ships. Only about eight Americans survived! My cousin was one of those that died in that bombing.

But when we were there, now eight years after the end of World War II, and their unconditional surrender to the US, the people treated us with respect and there was not one act of subterfuge on the part of the Japanese that I know of. I knew a different Japan, tiny and clean. Of course, a number of things had happened since WWII. I liked the Japanese people that I knew.

General Douglas MacArthur, who knew their culture very well, was instrumental in Japan's rise to a robust economy and a democratic government after World War II. I don't know whether he or President Roosevelt was responsible, at the beginning of the war, for abandoning an entire army which later surrendered and ended up in the infamous "Batton death march" or if the decision was the best they could do under the circumstances. War is terrible and sometime requires terrible decisions. For example, the atom bomb was a terribly hard decision and cost many Japanese lives, but brought an abrupt end to that terrible war and the cruel treatment of prisoners. In the end it saved many lives, especially American lives. Before each bomb, they told Japan what they would do and demanded their unconditional surrender. Japan refused. Only after the second bomb did they surrender.)

In the beginning of the war, when it became obvious that the Americans were not at all prepared for fighting the Japanese, MacArthur took his army to New Zealand where he prepared them for war, and when he came back, he showed military wisdom in winning that terrible war against all odds. Many American lives were lost in that terrible war to extricate the Japanese from all of those islands. They had spent 20 years in building underground fortresses, which made it very difficult to overcome them.

After Japan folded, he demanded a complete an unconditional surrender. To punctuate that fact and subdue the entire nation, on the day of the ceremony of their surrender, he lined up all the top brass of the Japanese military on the deck of a carrier. Starting with the highest ranks, and going down the line of officers, he ripped off their insignias of rank and medals and threw them on the deck and trampled on them. I thought when I saw the newsreel that he was humiliating them more than necessary. But as I began to understand the culture, I realized that the Japanese culture was very monolithic. They followed their leaders; to death, to wage war, or to surrender. <u>All of Japan</u> surrendered on that day. It also helped that the emperor, Hirohito, in a public appearance admitted that he was not God.

After that, McArthur had a strong influence in writing their constitution, which was copied from the USA model. The Marshall Plan and the Lend Lease program funded by the US went a long way to restore their broken country. He said, "I want a thousand missionaries to come to Japan!" Then came the Korean war, of which the cease-fire had just been signed when our Squadron landed there. Japan needed the protection of the US from the encroachment of Communism, as they had been completely disarmed after World War II. It now seemed that the II World War had never existed. We were friends!

All that to say that we, as military men, had a good relationship with the Japanese people. There seemed to be no animosity and they dearly liked our money that we spent there. We could move freely among the people. I wanted to see and taste the culture. I had the privilege of visiting inside several family houses. Everything is in miniature as compared with the US. And everything is super clean. Every house has a porch. It's very small with a bench on one side to sit while you take off your shoes. No shoes are allowed inside the house. The rooms were small and the walls made of thin wood. Between one house and another there was a small space, sometimes only about eight inches. The floor of the house was about three feet off the ground. In each room there was a tiny sliding door at floor level to open and sweep the dust out of the house. The dining living room had a table in the center about 12 inches off the floor and a leg space under the table for your feet and legs. In the winter they put a "hibachi" pot in the leg space filled with live coals to warm your feet and legs. The table cloth draped down over your legs made it a very comfortable place to sit. The family invited me to eat with them and warm my feet under their table. That meant that I was accepted as a guest. Even entering into the living room was an honor. From the porch you had to take off your shoes, but going on into the living room, you had to take off your socks as well.

The bathroom had no underground drain and the excrement fell into a tank or buckets underneath. We called them "honey buckets" They hauled it out daily to the farms and dumped it on the crops and gardens. Needless to say, the crops flourished. Our commanders told us it was alright to eat their food, but better not to eat lettuce or other above ground vegetables. Rice was their staple food. Their saying was "No more rice, pretty soon die!"

The electric train system in the Tokyo area was very efficient and on time, but only ran through the center of the city, so to reach the outlying parts of the city, you would use either the tiny taxi cars, or the bicycle rickshaws. The original rickshaw was pulled by a man on foot, but the rickshaw in Tokyo was a tricycle which had a seat wide enough for two small passengers, a roof and curtains to close during the winter with the ever-present hibachi pot to keep warm. The man on the bicycle had very strong legs and would take you anywhere in the city you wanted to go. The motor taxis seemed to be somewhat of a risk as there was no traffic control, they went as fast as they could, honking and swerving between other cars and the many people who shared the street as well. In spite of their seemingly wild driving, we didn't see any accidents.

The merchants were always friendly and businesslike. They loved to sell and would haggle with us over prices. I found that at closing time they were especially anxious to sell because they believed that if they made a sale right at closing time, then tomorrow would be a good day of business!

Men would pee on the streets. I don't know what the women did. The first time I went to Tokyo on the train, at the Central Station the men's bathroom was out of order, so men and women both used the women's bath room without hesitation. It seemed perfectly normal for them. We were beginning to see a great difference in our cultures. To them it was no big deal. I learned enough Japanese to get around, to buy things and in a basic way to make myself understood. Most Japanese knew some English as well. English was taught in schools even prior to World War II.

The Marine Air Base had been a World War II Japanese Base. Kamikaze pilots had taken off from this air base. It was situated in the midst of a farming area. The Base was divided in two parts by a deep valley with a dirt dike on which was our road connecting the two sides. On the one side was the barracks for our two Squadrons, the "guard" barracks, the mess hall, the clinic, the "slop shoot" (cafeteria and beer) and "outdoor movie" (wooden benches and screen) and the Main Gate. On the other side was the flight line and hangars where all the work and flying took place. The officer's quarters was there on the other side of the airstrip. When we crossed the dike to go to work, we could see on one side of the dike a small village and on the other side their little fields. There was a tunnel below where the farmers crossed each day to do their work. We could only see the roof tops in the village, but the farming side was interesting. They planted rice and vegetables. Each morning the farmers carried "honey buckets" suspended from a wooden yoke over their shoulders to spread on their fields. Each field was bordered by small dikes and the rice was submerged with water about half of the time. The fields were very neat with paths between each field. There wasn't a weed in sight.

Some of us would sometimes visit the Navy base in Yokosuka to go swimming there as they had a beautiful swimming pool. I learned to do the flip off the high board there, but when I came back to the States never continued practicing.

Kirby, Pierce and I spent several week-ends at what had been a vacation hotel for Japanese officers. It was taken over for a special services hotel for the US Military. The total cost including food was five or six dollars a day, super cheap. It was a huge hotel situated on a beautiful blue mountain lake with a view of the mount Fuji. The floors and walls were raw cement. Evidently all the luxury had been renovated, but the beds were comfortable and the food was good. I learned to water ski there. A Japanese man had an old boat with a worn-out Ford Motor. It didn't have power enough to pull a man up on skis, so we would sit on the dock with our feet on the skis in the water and hold on to the rope. He would go as fast as possible past the dock and when the boat hit the end of the rope, we would hopefully be able to get up on the skis before our weight slowed him down too much! We practically had that beautiful blue lake all to ourselves. The Japanese economy hadn't yet recovered to the point of national tourism, and for some reason, not many servicemen had found that beautiful resort. We sure had a lot of fun though.

CHAPTER FIVE
FUJIYAMA

Yama means mountain and its name is Fuji. A well-known saying is: "He who does not climb Fujiyama in a lifetime is a fool, but he who climbs it twice is a greater fool." Our squadron was going on an outing and this one was really special. We were to take two days and the entire group (perhaps nearly a hundred men) would climb the mountain. Fuji was formed by a volcano which had broken through the earth's crust in only one opening and formed a perfect cone shaped mountain. It rises 11,000 ft above sea level, but different from many mountain ranges in the world which have their "foot hills" that lead up gradually to their highest peaks. Fuji's base is 1000 ft, which means that to climb the mountain, you have to climb 10,000 ft. in one stretch. It's quite a climb. There is a trail, in fact it's a very well-worn trail as many thousands of tourists have made the climb. There are no particularly dangerous parts but it is very steep and requires lots of energy and stamina. Many mountains have shoulders and valleys which Fuji does not have.

We traveled by bus and then by train to a station close to the base of the mountain. It was a long trip. There was a lodge there. They told us it's a *must* to buy a walking staff. It was over six feet long. There are little huts on the trail at each 1000 ft. where they will brand your stick marking the altitude of that station. That way there is no question about how high you were able to climb. We started to climb at six in the afternoon. In nice weather, it normally takes 20 hours for someone in good shape to climb all the way to the top and come back.

When we started out, two other Marines and I right away took the lead. I was pretty confident I could out climb anybody. I weighed 160 pounds none of which was extra baggage. It soon started to rain, but we kept going. We overtook three young Japanese people and they joined us, two young men and a girl. The rain got harder, and progress was

extremely difficult as we would slip back at every step. But we didn't stop. We encouraged one another and there was more than a little competition. The rain was coming down in buckets now, but still undaunted, we kept climbing. We passed one station, two stations, three stations. At each they branded our sticks. The stations were very small stone huts with a fire for the branding iron and only room for the one or two people who attended it and maybe two "climbers", and we had to stoop to go in. They charged us a small fee for branding the stick. We lost all track of time. We had left the others far behind with not a thought about turning back.

But finally, my companions began to get discouraged. Well after midnight the girl and one of the Japanese boys decided to turn back. The downpour of rain had not abated, and though there was no wind to speak of, (on our side of the mountain), the trail was very slippery, making progress difficult. Finally, the two other Marines turned back. They said, "We haven't heard from our group for hours. Maybe they turned back? We might be AWOL, (absent without leave)." It must have been near dawn. I had a watch on but hadn't checked it for hours. It was under my wet clothing. Everything was soaking wet, so the rain couldn't get us any wetter. I said, "I'm not going to turn back." I didn't give a thought about a Court Marshal for being AWOL. The Japanese boy didn't want to be bettered by an American, so he stayed with me. But finally, he too, decided to turn back. We could still get our walking sticks branded. The people at the stations weren't going anywhere. It was daylight now but dim because of the clouds and rain.

When I got to the ten-thousand-foot station, I stopped to rest. The hut was larger and had a table. They offered me some food. It was squishy squid, which I ate. I was very hungry and besides, one of my mottoes was to try a little of everything. The attendant from the top station was there as well. He had come down because he said the wind was so terribly strong from the other side of the mountain. They tried to convince me not to go on alone, but when they saw they couldn't persuade me, they put the last brand of eleven thousand feet on my stick. (He had brought the iron down with him.) They warned me to be very careful. The wind is extremely dangerous, they said. So, I went up the last 1,000 feet with the dire warnings and knowing that if I should fall or the wind blow me off the mountain, no one would know it. Advancing was extremely difficult and slow. The last 1000 feet was extremely steep. At every step I slipped back almost as much as I advanced. I wanted to look down into the crater. The rain was abating now. At least I could see more than just three feet in front of me.

The top of the mountain! I made it! But I couldn't see over the rim yet. I had come to what was like a tiny street, carved out of the rock, about ten yards long. Carving out the street had made a wall about four feet high, all solid rock. There were several caves, carved out of the rock wall, the eleven-thousand-foot station was one of them, and there was an altar to Buda, and I looked inside. The opening had bars to prevent people from getting in. There was a candle or some kind of light burning in front of a little Buda.

There were steps carved into the rock wall that reached the rim, but when I stuck my head above the rim, I found out maybe why the others had turned back. I have never, before or since, encountered such a strong wind. I found out later that a hurricane had been pounding the other side of the mountain all night! The squadron had been ordered to turn back shortly after they started out. The trail had been closed. It was prohibited to go any further, but we didn't know that. Had I known it was a hurricane, I don't know if I would have ventured to buck the wind to see down into the crater. I had to crawl on my belly to make it over to the edge and look down. I couldn't see very far down. It had stopped raining though. About 1,000 feet down were some clouds and on one side a slide had formed a sort of shelf there. Satisfied that I had made my goal and though I didn't have a camera to take a picture, I said, "Well I'm here and I and myself know that!"

I began to take my bearings and decide what to do now. I looked at my watch; a quarter till four in the afternoon! I couldn't believe it! The train would leave at five. I didn't have that much time to make it back down to make the train! Now I began to worry about what my superiors would say to me. The others surely had turned back. They probably have all gone back to the Base! I estimated how far the trail had traversed across the mountain and estimated where the Lodge would be. Not far from where I had come out on top, the mountain had a side that was loose shale and it was in the lee of the mountain, out of the wind. I estimate that I could just about come out near the station if I took a course straight down. Of course, it was strictly prohibited to attempt to go up or down on that side as it is very dangerous. I didn't give it a thought. Using my stick as a rudder, I started down. I leaned way back on the stick, almost laying down and began to slide. I lifted one foot and then the other, taking giant steps, perhaps up to ten yards each time. Though this side of the mountain was out of the wind, I was going so fast that the wind was whistling around my ears! After about five minutes my legs would start to tremble from the extreme exertion so I would lie down and plow to a stop and rest a bit. (The danger of course was that this would start a slide that would take me and tons of shale all the way down the mountain, or that I would lose my balance and go head over heels down the mountain.) I had to rest about two or three times on the way down, and on the trip, ground my stick off about two feet, but I made it down in just over fifteen minutes! That's about 8 miles an hour even with rest stops!

The train would leave at 5 PM. our group was gone and there was no way I could make it back to the Base that night. I called my sergeant. I expected it to be bad, but I had to call him. To my surprise, all he said was, "Oh there you are!" I told him I made it to the top. He said, "You get your -—back here!" Then I heard him say something to someone behind him. They laughed. Back on the phone he said, "You can stay overnight at Army Base …" (I don't remember the name) which was not too far from where I was and the train passed right by the main gate. My clothes had dried quickly from body heat after the rain stopped, and I just had time to catch the train! They evidently called ahead to let them know that I would be staying the night there, because when I presented my ID at the Main Gate, they let me right in and told me where to go.

To my happy surprise, there was a small detachment of Marines there, and I found an old buddy of mine that I hadn't seen for a long time. This Army Base was pure luxury compared to our Marine Base. The Marine base was an old Japanese air base, and three hundred and sixty men of the two squadrons of Marines were housed in the two wings of that old World War II barracks. The cement floor was deteriorated and really rough to sweep. Eight men had double bunk beds in a space approximately 18 feet by 11 feet. That included the lockers which separated one "bedroom" from another. The four racks (double bunks) were arranged in such a way to leave a very small "living" space just big enough for a card table. The barracks was a long open building with these "bedrooms" lining each side. A hallway separated the two wings. At the end by the hallway there was a small room fenced off with woven wire that we used to store sports equipment and where about six of us would work out with weights every other day. We had a small bench that we used to do the bench press. There was a low spot in the middle of the floor and it would fill with sweat as we worked out! We drank gallons of water every day in that humid climate!

But this Army Base had new buildings! And the large open bays with big windows where the men slept was to me like a luxury hotel! I was able to take a shower. Each man had a single cot with lots of space all around it! And the food! I'll never forget the taste of fresh eggs the next morning! At our Base, we ate powdered eggs, and though we got nourished well enough, the powdered eggs always smelled a little bit rotten! My old Marine buddy and I compared a lot of experiences since we had last seen each other. But the next morning I had to get back on the road so we bade goodbye and I left. We never saw each other again.

That's the way it is in the Military, a lot of separations. But it's much worse when the unit is in actual combat.

CHAPTER SIX
ACCIDENTS

We were proud of our outfit and most of us felt responsible to keep our planes in top condition. However, the fighter jets were complicated machines, and many different things could happen even with the best of maintenance. However, there were a couple of the guys who felt they could get through life without working. Leadership has a lot to do with it too. Our line sergeant was a man that I had little respect for. He never left his desk to check on what was happening on the flight line and worse yet, he had his favorites. I perhaps wouldn't even remember him, because most of my superiors and officers, I held in great respect. But something happened that to me was a disgrace to the Corps and perhaps changed the course of my life.

But first I will recount some "normal" accidents. One of our jobs was fixing tires. The two main tires on the FJ2 were about the size of a small truck tire but carried 220 pounds of air pressure because these fighter planes, weighing several tons, touched down at about 250 miles an hour! The tires were 12 ply and of first quality hard rubber. The wheels were made to part in half for changing tires. They were held together by 16 bolts. Sometimes the pilots would come in too hard and blow out a tire as they hit the deck, even though those tires would take quit a blow. One new pilot nervously locked his brakes as he came in and blew out both tires, since the aircraft was not slowing down as it should, he pressed down harder. Both tires caught on fire! When he finally got stopped, he had ground off nearly half of both wheels as well! Fortunately, no other damage was done.

One day two of my fellow line men were attempting to change a tire. The last bolt was really stubborn and they had worked most of the morning on that stubborn bolt! They finally decided to take it into the metal shop to have it cut off. When they dropped it on the floor, it exploded and blew the top half of the wheel through the roof of the metal shop! Luckily, no one was hurt. They had forgotten to let out the 220 pounds of air pressure! Human error? But the line sergeant was sitting at his desk in the same room and didn't realize what the problem was.

PLANE DOWN! Mayday! Mayday1 A night fighter coming back from a night mission in the early morning hours, broke the radio silence at the tower with that urgent message. They had been doing surveillance over the "38th parallel" the buffer zone between North and South Korea. They must have taken a hit. Before the tower could get a second bead on them, their radio went off. If the tower can get two compass readings on the plane, they can calculate a triangle that will give them an approximate point where the plane last gave out a signal and the direction of the plane. But they didn't get that second bead, so that started a week of intensive search. Our search was mostly on the sea and our hopes were that the two pilots had bailed out and were in an inflatable raft. It was a terrible week, made much worse because it was extremely cloudy and the visibility was very low, and because of a false signal that sounded like the little emergency radio that comes packed in each life raft. The signal was very weak, but they thought perhaps the radio had suffered damage and for that reason was giving out a weak signal. It was a risky decision, but the life of the two men on board was at stake, so search, we must!

The fog made searching extremely difficult. A search helicopter went down at sea with four men on board. Two men were lost. Then, four planes were flying low and parallel in order to cover a wider strip of the sea. In the fog, they suddenly came to an island rising out of the sea. Three planes were able to peel up and off, the other did not, crashing into the mountain.

A Navy destroyer joined the search with men on board scanning the sea. The radio signal continued. It was very weak but understandable in those circumstances. The signal they were hearing in Morse code indicated that the men on the raft could see the ship. In code, they asked,

"Is the ship within a mile of your raft?" The answer was affirmative. "Is it within a thousand yards?" Affirmative! "Is it within 500 yards?" Affirmative! All eyes of the men on board were craning to catch sight of the raft. Nothing! "Is it within 300 yards?" Affirmative! Nothing in sight! "Is it within 100 yards?" Affirmative! "Can you see the men on board?" Affirmative! <u>That must be a false signal!</u>

They found out that the Commies had set up a small radio transmitter in a cove near the shore that sent the signal out to sea, making it appear to be coming from somewhere out at sea! The downed plane was never found and unfortunately three men were lost, plus a plane and a helicopter in the search! It was a very sad week! But why? Because Americans value the lives of their fellows, and we will always do what we can to save them!

MIRACLE LANDING One of my favorite pilots was taking off. I can't remember his name but we'll call him Captain Steward. Just after he lifted off, he had a flame out (engine failure). That would be at least 230 miles an hour. He was nearing the end of our short air strip and it would not be possible to circle and land again. Beyond the paved air strip there were about 50 yards of muddy ground, then a ditch, a road and a fence. On the other side of the fence was a rice paddy which was many feet lower. The rice paddy was full of water at that moment.

Captain Steward was a crack pilot and one of our lead pilots as well. He cramped his plane down near the end of the runway and plowed through the remaining 50 yards of mud, then hit the ditch which caused his plane to nose dive and the last we saw was the tail of the plane high in the air as it flipped over the fence. Fire trucks and ambulance with sirens screaming took the shortest route they could find to get to the scene of the crash. We stood on the NC5's, (generator and towing units for starting and towing the planes) but couldn't see a thing beyond the hole in the fence.

When news got back to the flight line, we were relieved to find out that Captain Steward was unhurt miraculously. The plane had landed on

its back in the water of the rice paddy and then done another flip and landed on its wheels! When the ambulance got there, he was leaning on the side of the plane smoking a cigarette! However, in his next accident, Captain Steward was not so fortunate.

CHAPTER SEVEN
THE GAMBLING VICE

Many of the guys gambled. I tried it a few times but decided it wasn't for me. The last time I gambled was playing pinocle. I liked the game and had played it before many times just for fun. We decided that we would play for a penny a point. That sounded reasonable and I couldn't lose too much money. I was highly mistaken. In just a very short time, I lost about $18 dollars! That was almost a third of my pay for 15 days! I was already seeing how much some of the guys were losing. My bunkmate was one of them. He was pretty young because he lied about his age and got in early. That might be beside the point of gambling but I think his immaturity didn't help him to see what was happening to him. He was from Wyoming and it seemed that in the winter months they didn't have much else to do but gamble. He was always talking about his brother-in-law that always was winning so much money. It seemed that gambling was about all this kid was living for! And he was broke all the time!

As I said, our cubical where we slept had just enough room for a card table with bunk beds all around. The guys would sit on the bunks and play cards every spare moment. I soon saw that gambling soon becomes a vice, but, where did the money go? My buddies certainly weren't ending up with it! They were always broke! I decided to check it out and find out who was ending up with all that money every payday! So, I followed it through.

Payday was every 15 days and some of the guys were ever anxious for payday to come so they could get in that big game again. Observing "from a distance", I saw that it was pure stupidity, but many were "hooked" on it. We got off work at 4:30 or 5:00. Some of those guys would get right into a game when they got off work on payday and not even go to chow (eat). At 10:00PM the lights went out in the barracks, but those who still had money would move into the head (bathroom) where the lights stayed on all night. By that time some of them had either quit from a little good sense or had run out of money. The games would be getting hotter now. Those who were left had been winning! No chairs or table of course in the "head". They sat on the floor!

At first, there would be probably two or three groups playing. As time went on, more would drop out until finally there was only one group. The stakes getting higher all the time. About two or three in the morning one or two of the older guys from the guard barracks would come in. They were in charge of the gate and Base security. Many of them had re-enlisted, perhaps just to stay there and gamble? Anyway, they were older. They were always very gentlemanly and polite, observing from a distance for a while. When one of the "dummies" would drop out, one would say, "Do you all mind if I join you?" After playing for a while and sometimes losing, he would say "Can we up the ante a little?" Hot and winning, the dummies would say, "you bet, let's go!" Those guys were not dishonest; they were only smarter, more patient and <u>had a lot more money</u> to deal with!

A simple truth is that a dummy gambler will not quit while he is winning, so all you need to beat him out of his money is patience and a lot more money than he has! So, the ante is upped and maybe the dummy wins! Let's up the ante again! Until finally the dummy, hot and winning goes for winner takes all! His "luck" finally runs out and he loses the pile! Nothing to do now but go to bed and dream about "if I'd just had luck, I could have won that pile and had it all!" The funny thing about it was, the same scenario happened every fifteen days!

So where does Robert F come into the picture? "He's always got money! I'll borrow five or ten from him till payday to buy some shaving cream and cigarettes, and have a sandwich and a beer in the evening. He only charges 50% and the others charge double, so I'll borrow from him." Well, Robert F stacked up quite a pile of money till the sergeant major found out about the "system". He said, "I've been told that some are lending money for interest! I'm not going to name names at this point, but I don't want to hear any more about it! So that stopped my sweet deal, but I already had accumulated quite a nice amount of money. I already had bought my mother a ninety-seven piece set of the famous Narataki China.

CHAPTER EIGHT
THE CAMPAIGN FOR PILOTS

The First Marine Air Wing of which we were a part, had a push for new pilots. Several guys, including Kirby and I, decided to try out for officer and pilot training, which would take place in Pensacola, Florida. The school and training would last 18 months and those that passed would come out as second lieutenants and pilots with a commitment of two and a half more years, four years in total. I thought that would be "fun" to be a fighter pilot. I liked anything daring and I loved to fly. The entry exams and physical was a long process. It took us about six months at least.

The first part of the screening process was the physical. In my case, the doctor who gave me the physical was a dead pan (showed no emotions). I went in, went through all the exercises and tests without one comment from the doctor, except that he didn't pass me! In about two weeks he would call me in again. Each time the exercise part was more strenuous and longer, but still no comment. I had to run on a treadmill, climb stairs and do pushups. I wasn't one to ask either, so was somewhat in the dark about what he was thinking. Kirby and the others past that part with flying colors. I was a bit mystified. I felt good. I surely couldn't be that I was failing the physical!? But I didn't say anything to anyone.

Finally on the third time after the doc had finished, he called me to his desk and said, "I was very puzzled about the results of your tests because your heart does not respond normally to extreme exercise. I thought, either this man is almost dead, or he is in stronger and better condition than anyone I've ever tested before. I've found that the latter is true! You have clean bill of health! Good luck to you!" I ask him why he thought my heart was so unusual. He said, "You have an abnormally large and strong heart. In your case it may be because of very extreme exercise in sports or something during your formative years." I hadn't participated much in sports because of farm work, but as I thought back, I remembered how when irrigating on a sandy hill the gofer holes would many times cause the water to break out and in a short time, the hole would get very large to the point of taking all the water in the ditch down the sandy hill! I would fight those breakouts with a fury, not willing to ever give up shoveling until I had plugged up the breakout. I started irrigating by myself when I was about 14. That's what had caused my heart to grow unusually?

Knowing that we were trying out for NAVCADS, (Navy Cadets) and that now only Kirby and I were still eligible from our outfit, an honest and candid officer called us apart one day and talked to us at great length. In spite of his fame, he was a very humble and approachable officer. He was a holder of the NAVY CROSS, the highest honor that the Navy can give to someone who has been in combat. It is given mostly to dead heroes! The story behind his medal was that in World War II he was flying a Corsair, a gull winged propeller driven fighter which became rapidly popular when it came out towards the end of the war because of its outstanding maneuverability. James* and his buddy had been in a "dog fight" with Japanese Zero's. They had shot down all but one and they both ran out of ammunition. The remaining Zero was closing in on the tail of his buddy. James did a fancy flip to the side and came in on the tail of the Zero, deliberately ramming him with his propeller and managed to chop up the tail causing the Zero to lose control and go down. James was also an "ace" for the number of zeros he had shot down. Pilots like him who faced danger and death on every mission, were instrumental in helping win that terrible war. He was very modest and didn't talk about his WWII record, but his interest in talking to us was that we should know what we were getting in to if we became pilots. He laid out all the pros and cons honestly so that we could decide for ourselves.

My attitude toward military service in general and the Marine Corps especially, was good. I sincerely felt that military service was a good thing for any young man, and that defending our country and defending freedom in the world was necessary. I had volunteered for the Marine Corps to be able to choose my branch of service. I was especially proud of the "Corps" as we affectionately called it. "Semper Fi" was our call word and still is. It means, "Always Faithful"

However, when Captain James told us that the Corps was kind of in a slump, I could see that. Leadership is so important, and when he told us that at that moment there was not a very high moral standard among the junior officers. I could see that. There were several officers that I admired greatly, himself included. But some things had happened that I didn't admire at all. Only two will I mention, and they both happened after he talked to us. The pilots that took us to Hong Kong were found taking drugs back to Japan was one of them. Also, one night two drunk lieutenants came in to our barracks with a stolen pig they wanted someone to butcher for them. In both cases, I thought it was conduct unfit for and officer. I was somewhat idealistic, and that was the conduct of a few among many, but it was a negative.

The other negative was what was happening in our line shack. The line sergeant was not a good leader. The accident with the wheel that exploded should have been caught by him. They had been fighting with that wheel all morning in the same line shack where he had his desk. Also, he had a favorite, Napolitano. Napolitano was one of those guys that figured he could get through life without working. He had a buddy under his wing that was following in his footsteps.

The line sergeant was married and every day, he sat at his desk in the line shack and wrote several pages of letter to his wife. Every night he went off base to live with his Japanese concubine. He never went out on the flight line to inspect the work. Several serious things happened because of his lack of leadership. These things didn't really bother me all that much at the time. I just registered them in my mind. It was later that I saw how it all added up to a very bad incident.

But I continued with the process of examinations. After the physical was the mental aptitude tests which were quite complete and even rigid.

Three of the guys had failed on the written test. Now Kirby was having trouble with the eye test. He had a habit of reading by flashlight after the lights were out at night, so he stopped that and started drinking a lot of carrot juice, but in the end couldn't pass. My eyes were fine but my hearing was marginal. So, they sent me to Hong Kong on R&R to rest up my hearing! They knew that on the flight line where we worked, we were subject to the torturing sounds of jets "turning up". We used no ear protection and all day long, the jets were turning up and pulling out, just feet from where we were standing. Then there were the engine shop tests. When they completed a 100-hour inspection of an engine, they turned it up to 100%. They usually did that in the evening when we would be off duty. Our movie theater was out doors, with wood benches for the viewers. Though the hangers were across a valley, when the engine shop would test an engine, the roar of a jet turning up to 100% was such that you couldn't hear the movie. In fact, you could shout at the top of your voice to the man sitting next to you and he wouldn't hear a thing! All that probably didn't help anybody's hearing!

So, they sent me to Hong Kong to rest my hearing. Ever ready for adventure, I was ready to go! The guys who had been to Hong Kong told me you could buy tailored clothing and other things there, very cheap. That sounded good, and I had gathered a nice "nest egg" from my erstwhile loaning operation.

CHAPTER NINE
HONG KONG

HONG KONG was independent of China at that time. Great Britain had leased it for ninety-nine years and it was under their supervision. It was at that time a free port; <u>all trade was legal and no taxes</u>. They said it was the only completely free port in the world at that time. (Great Britain's lease ran out in the 1980's.) It is a very interesting city consisting in two parts, Kowloon which was on the mainland and the island of Hong Kong which was filled with world banks. In spite of the fact that *everything* was legal, and that perhaps no other place in the world at that time had such an influx of immigrants (mostly from China and India) as they had, it was a clean city. Bustling with all kinds of businesses.

Our group of servicemen on R&R stayed in a hotel well adapted for us. Most people there spoke English. The hotel was cheap for us and they put on a special 17 course dinner one night, with the host explaining about each dish. The dinner took about two hours and it wasn't overfilling! Many of the dishes were "bitter-sweet", a Chinese specialty, a kind of candied seafood dish. It was an interesting and enjoyable experience.

We were welcomed everywhere we went. Of course, they wanted to sell us their wares! I bought three tailored suits, a top coat and a sports jacket, all of cashmere cloth made from a combination of llama and sheep wool. I also bought five leather suitcases, each made to store inside the next larger one so that you can carry them all in one big suitcase, and a teakwood coffee table. Many of the business men in the city were from India. The tailor from whom I bought the clothing loaned us his Mercedes Benz car with chauffeur to tour the city and go up the "lookout mountain" to get a beautiful view of the city and across the border into Communist China!

We had climbed a very high hill. You could call it a mountain. Of course, we were on the side belonging to Hong Kong. The city was below us. On the other side of the deep valley was China. There was a river flowing through the valley. The entire side of that mountain was covered with rice paddies. Each little paddy was leveled with a dike around it. There were trails up the mountain between the rice paddies. Men were carrying water in buckets hung from a yoke across the shoulders of each man. I thought, what a life! Do they spend their whole life carrying water up that mountain? I have no idea if there was another source of water higher up the mountain but at least part of it was carried like that. That must be their life! Carrying water every day!

I thought at the time that it was totally because of ignorance that these people are limited or condemned to doing this all their lives. I later found out that education alone does not lift people up. They need freedom!

Many of the men on military leave caroused in the bars at night, but I was too busy buying and taking in the culture of that amazing city! Another Marine and I got to know an American family with two girls that was touring the world! They bought us a good Steak dinner, which we enjoyed immensely and then said thank you!

The Rickshaw was more genuine here than in Japan. The men who pulled them evidently had spent their entire lives doing that because they had huge legs and small arms and torso. I took one several times. They warned us though, to be very careful and not go into small alleys. They can flip the two wheeled rickshaw back and bump your head and they fight with their very powerful legs to overcome their victim and rob him. I had no trouble.

We ate fish dinner one night on the island of Hong Kong. The road circles around the big banks to the other side of the island where there is a small bay very well protected from the sea and storms where the little fishing boats can port to sell their fish and buy supplies to go out to sea again. The bay, about a half mile across was full, literally full of fishing boats. I thought, how does one get out of here if they are near the shore with a couple hundred yards of boats in his way? I soon found out. A family on a boat near where I was standing wanted to leave. They began to shout and their neighbors began to shout and miraculously a narrow path opened up for them to go out into the larger bay, and I suppose out to sea for however long a time they would spend out there fishing, catching crabs or whatever they do.

We decided to eat at a special "restaurant" on that bay. It was a boat, medium size and firmly docked. On the water side was a big net with all kinds of sea food alive! We picked out what we wanted and the waiter caught it up in a net. Then we sat down and waited for our very fresh fish dinner!

We spent about five days in Hong Kong; I had sent all my "goodies" back to the States by military mail. The merchants with expertise, made the packages and I put our home address on them. Uncle Sam takes them free of charge to the US Post Office in California, and we pay the postage from there.

Back on Base in Japan, they sent me to the big Naval hospital in Yokosuka to re-take my hearing test. Very much more sophisticated than the former test I had taken at the Base where there were all the noises of the flight line. We went down to about the third basement into a very soundproof room. Without any outside noises, I passed the test fine. Although I personally held some reserves about whether I could hear that well when I would be in flight with all the noises and static that there would be. My hearing apparatus evidently does not filter out other sounds, making a jumble in my head so I can't understand what is being said. But technically I had passed, so all was in order to go before the FIRST MARINE AIR WING Board in Seoul, South Korea for the officers there to check me out. It would be a formality. They told me that in no way would they reject me. As it turned out, I was the only one out of the entire First Marine Air Wing that had passed everything!

However, Captain James council had made me think twice about becoming a pilot! He explained that the training was good, but politics had gotten in to the Corps and the moral level of the pilots was fairly low at that point in time. That was impressed on my mind when one night I happened to see a movie that depicted a pilot who had been called back into service from civilian life because he was in the reserves. He was quite bitter about it. It made me think of that possibility. If we signed up for NAVCADS, we would have eighteen months of training, then two and a half years of service. I was alright with that. But they told us that we would be in the reserves as long as we were able bodied. I wanted to get out of the service and go back to the farm which I loved and my enlistment time was getting close. All those things put together were influencing my prospective.

CHAPTER TEN
THE TURNING POINT

NIAGATA was in northern Japan. We were there for gunnery practice. Periodically the pilots have to practice their expertise in gunnery and it must be of course in a desert area or over the sea. In this case off the coast of northern Japan. We didn't get to watch the show of their practice, but I was looking forward to their formation take-off and flight when they would leave to go back to our home base.

Our planes, the FJ2, used a removable "tip tank" that could be attached to the underside of each wing to carry extra fuel for long flights. During combat the tanks could be replaced with bombs. During the gunnery practice, neither bombs nor fuel tanks were attached in order to give the plane more maneuverability. Now in getting ready for the long flight back to our home base, we had to re-attach the tip tanks. Each tank carried 200 gallons of fuel, that's about 1300 pounds hanging from two small pincer like attachments made of molybdenum, a very high strength metal. It goes without saying that the tanks should be attached securely with utmost care.

Each plane captain was responsible for the flight readiness of his plane. My plane was number seven. Most of the men were diligent about taking care of their planes, but Napolitano was one of those guys trying to get through life without working or by working very little. He and his buddy played around all morning and when it was almost time for takeoff, they coaxed several other guys to help them hook up their tip tanks and fill them with jet fuel in a big hurry.

The flights were scheduled to go out four at a time in beautiful formation. With 24 planes, that meant six flights, four at a time and one right after another, quiet and awesome air show. The first four planes lined up in a staggered formation. Captain Steward had the lead plane of the first group He was on the right nearest to the flight line where we worked at refueling and maintenance. He had drawn Napolitano's plane. I was watching intently because my plane was in that flight and because I so much loved to watch the matchless precision of the pilots in this difficult maneuver. To my dismay, soon after they started moving, the nose of the right-hand tip tank on his plane dropped to the ground and began to produce fiery sparks! Captain Steward didn't realize it because he as lead man was looking over his left shoulder and back part of the time to the other planes.

Evidently the other pilots didn't see the sparks because they were behind and to the left. I felt paralyzed with no way to communicate with the tower or the pilot. The fiery sparks got worse and worse. As he lifted off, the nose of the heavy tip tank dropped further down and its tail came up, forcing the right aileron on the plane to flip up, causing the wing to twist to the right and hit the ground. He brought the plane down hard. The tank was now enveloped in flames. He jettisoned (loosed) the tanks and his canopy. Plane and tanks went over the hill in flames. The plane, now out of sight, plowed to a stop and the tip tanks crossed in front of the plane leaving two paths of fire. One went right through a village house. Luckily it hit no one.

The pilot was injured. His back was hurt and he was in a daze. A quick-thinking Marine was walking on a road that was parallel to the path of the plane. When he saw the plane go down, he ran like mad to help the pilot. When he got there the pilot was dazedly turning off switches. He was able to pull him out to safety before the plane blew up. (I have a picture of the burned-out skeleton). We heard that Captain Steward's back was injured. That accident was <u>caused</u> and should have been judged, but to the shame of our outfit, Napolitano was not only able to get out of work but also get out of being punished. The line sergeant was also responsible. He should have personally inspected that crucial and important process of re-attaching those tip-tanks. I think that was the last straw so to speak that convinced me not to go to NavCad's for flight training. (Not because of the danger, but that this episode turned my stomach.) I still loved the Corps, but this whole thing really upset me. Very soon after that incident I had to decide whether to get into the program of pilot training

As they flew us back to Home Base, I was brooding, because I knew that Napolitano was a favorite of the line Sergeant. I had little respect for that particular Sergeant. He was living unfaithful to his wife while he sat in the line shack every morning writing a long letter of love to her. Besides, he was not provided leadership to his men. When we got back to Home Base, they called all the mechanics "on the carpet" and bawled us out royally for extreme "negligence" that cost the government millions and could have cause the death of a pilot. I thought to myself, "This accident has a name attached to it. Each one of us has a plane assigned to maintain in order. This is not a group problem, it's a problem of two men in particular, Napolitano and his buddy!"

While I was thinking all that, I knew that to say anything would cause uproar. The line Sergeant could be implicated as well and he would spare nothing to make this a "group problem". Was I afraid to speak up the truth? The line Sergeant would most certainly back up Napolitano. My conscience has bothered me many times since then. The Marine Corps has a good name, and that is not an accident, but a result of diligence and courage. I was also letting the Corps down! But there was another reason I didn't say anything and maybe it was just an excuse. I was due to be discharged in just one month and I wanted to get out and go back to farming. So, I kept my mouth shut, bowed my head and said nothing. Nobody else said anything either. Many of us knew where the problem was.

Soon they called me in to tell me I was elected to go before the Headquarters of the First Marine Air Wing in Korea for the final oral examine, which they assured me would only be routine because they were quite proud to have a man eligible to go through the flight training program. I knew their hopes were high. All the battery of physical and mental tests were quite rigid to elect from among the enlisted men new officers and pilots! And now only one had made it through. But I had made up my mind. As I said, the incident of the tip tank and subsequent plane crash had soured me at that point. I said, "No, I'm not going!" The officers were very gentlemanly and didn't insist. It never occurred to me that they thought the accident and the danger involved had me scared out. That didn't even occur to me.

CHAPTER ELEVEN
SAN FRANCISCO
THE GOLDEN GATE BRIDGE!

It was very early in the morning but many of us were on deck. Today we arrive at San Francisco! It would be about two weeks of processing but many of us would soon be civilians again! I can't describe my feelings there at the railing of the ship straining to see that great Golden Gate Bridge that to us represented the United States of America and all that it stands for! The beauty and the majesty of that bridge does mighty credit to all that it represents!

Through the fog now we could barely make out the silhouette of the bridge in the early dawn light. Beautiful! But our ship is very large and stands high above the water! Will it go under the bridge? But I didn't realize we still had a couple of hours before we would get to the bridge. As we progressed, the bridge got bigger and bigger and bigger! When we finally passed under the bridge, our ship was like a little toy way down below that mighty bridge! I thought, "This is America! The land of the free and the home of the brave!! I love it!" **Little did I know that one day there would be a rot that would come in and almost consume that beautiful city!**

I always liked to volunteer for work that would keep me busy during the processing time, but this time I didn't have to volunteer. They put me on Shore Patrol right away. We patrolled the rough part of town. We went out each night in a team of four, two Sailors and two Marines. Our concern was not for civilians, unless it involved a service man. The area we covered was not too large, but filled with bars and brothels. We split up two and two but had radio communication. Mostly our work was about stopping fights and usually the men would calm down quickly when they saw the SP (Shore Patrol) arm band. Our "side arm" was a billy club, but you can do a lot of damage in a hurry with one of those. I soon found out that speaking in a low voice with authority and a firm grip on his arm got results a lot better than shouting. Most incidents we could solve that way. Only once did we have to call in the "paddy wagon" and take two guys in. Once they were locked in the wagon, we were free to go about our business. The guards on the paddy wagon were big bruisers and could easily handle those guys. The process was simple if there was no claim of property damage; dump them in the "cooler" all night and let them go in the morning!

I had a fright the first time I went to town with another guy in his car. He did a "U" at a filling station and came out on the right side of the road! In Japan they drive on the left and suddenly I was disoriented and thought we were in the wrong lane against the traffic. I yelled, "Lookout! you're on the wrong side of the road!" He said, "Calm down, this is US of A!"

I was discharged in San Francisco and given severance pay plus mileage to my home in Colorado. So, pockets "full of money", I decided to see the country. Not a thought of calling home! Back then it was legal to hitch hike and many people would pick up a young man in uniform. I hitch hiked to Los Angeles and visited an aunt. When I went to travel again, my goal was to see more of the country and I was happy to go wherever the people were going! I don't remember exactly how it happened but a family picked me up that was on vacation and going to Yosemite National Park. That would be going back north towards San Francisco! I had a great time with them and enjoyed seeing that beautiful park. They had two daughters too! Bidding them goodbye, I headed back towards Los Angeles but ended up veering off to the east, sleeping wherever night found me, usually in a YMCA, or if it was a small town, in a cheap hotel where I could take a shower.

I made it up to the edge of the great Grand Canyon, then back to the main route towards home in Colorado. A pair of homosexuals picked me up. They were nice enough, but had a rather weird philosophy about life and creation. I didn't feel very comfortable with them though and was glad when they let me off. I ended up going through the Rocky Mountains with a business man in a new Buick. He lived on the western slope and drove to Denver each week. His speedometer read close to 100 most of the time! It took me about two weeks to get home, no big deal. By now they were used to me not communicating! I hadn't told anyone when I got released so they didn't know that I was on the road.

"Home" was different now. Dad had sold the house and property at the edge of town for a good price, when the new highway went through there. He had been through some hard years after we three boys had gone to the service, and dry years had forced him out of farming. It seemed that now at last, "Good Fortune" was smiling on him! But, looking back, I think that many hardships had brought him to begin to seek the Lord, and the Lord was responding. He invested in a 22-acre tract with plans to build houses there. He had just finished a new house for the family, and wanted Willis and I to join him in the construction business. But we had plans to farm. We had learned the love of the soil from him! So, we formed a loose partnership, (meaning that each would have his own machinery, so that the partnership could be disbanded very easily. This was according to Dad's good council.) We rented a bunch of land and moved in to the little house on one of the farms we rented.

Willis didn't like to cook and I very soon got tired of cooking and began to think about marrying a good cook! (It would be nice to have a companion sweeter than my brother Willis also!) It was hard work that year. The three farms were far apart and the landlords of the one farm were very hard to please. We did have good crops and got a start with machinery. I bought a nearly new tractor and car. Willis bought a new tractor. He and I separated our loose partnership after that first year, though we worked together a lot after that. So, he farmed the old home place (240) and I the 22 acres that Dad was going to develop for a new neighborhood.

My attitude was like: Look out world, here I come! I've been through school (high school), I've been through the Marines, and I am confident that I can do about anything now! My brother Merv was going to college and he encouraged me to go. I said, I don't need that! I'm smart enough already! He said, yes, but college can prepare you better. I said, Nope, I'm good! Actually, I wasn't against studying. I had diligently studied agriculture by mail while I was in the service, and the GI Bill offered a good program for veterans to study, but I was in too much of a hurry to study. In my next book, Adventures in Faith I find the wife of my life, go from boom to bust, then find the real purpose of life! Hope to see you there!

Also by Robert F Paden

The Life and Times of Robert F Paden
The Kid From Kansas in the Marine Corps

Standalone
Deception in Perilous Times
The Glorious Church The Bride